Community Helpers

Mail Carriers

by Cari Meister

Bullfrog Books

Ideas for Parents and Teachers

Bullfrog Books let children practice reading informational text at the earliest reading levels. Repetition, familiar words, and photo labels support early readers.

Before Reading
- Discuss the cover photo. What does it tell them?
- Look at the picture glossary together. Read and discuss the words.

Read the Book
- "Walk" through the book and look at the photos. Let the child ask questions. Point out the photo labels.
- Read the book to the child, or have him or her read independently.

After Reading
- Prompt the child to think more. Ask: How does your mail carrier bring you the mail? What kinds of mail come in your mailbox?

Bullfrog Books are published by Jump!
5357 Penn Avenue South
Minneapolis, MN 55419
www.jumplibrary.com

Library of Congress Cataloging-in-Publication Data
Meister, Cari.
  Mail carriers / by Cari Meister.
    pages cm. —(Bullfrog books. Community helpers)
  Includes bibliographical references and index.
  Summary: "This photo-illustrated book for early readers gives examples of tasks postal service workers do and different places where mail carriers deliver the mail"—Provided by publisher.
  Audience: Grades K-3.
  ISBN 978-1-62031-077-9 (hardcover: alk. paper)
  ISBN 978-1-62496-033-8 (ebook)
1. Letter carriers—Juvenile literature. I. Title.
HE6241.M45 2014
383'.145--dc23
                                    2012044152

Series Editor: Rebecca Glaser
Series Designer: Ellen Huber
Book Designer: Lindaanne Donohoe
Photo Researcher: Rebecca Pettiford

Photo Credits: 123RF, 21; Alamy, 10, 16, 17; Corbis, 6, 7; Dreamstime, 4, 5, 22; iStockphoto, 1, 3, 4, 8, 9, 11, 12, 13, 14, 15, 18, 20, 23bl, 23br, 23tl; Shutterstock, cover, 6, 16, 19, 23tr, 24

Printed in the United States of America at Corporate Graphics in North Mankato, Minnesota.
5-2013 / PO 1003
10 9 8 7 6 5 4 3 2 1

Table of Contents

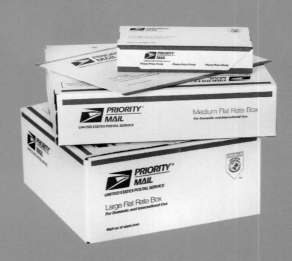

Mail Carriers at Work

Josh wants to be a mail carrier.
What do they do?

They bring mail to people.

UNITED STATES
POSTAL SERVICE

1052

Bob starts at the
post office.

He sorts mail.

9

Ben puts mail in bins.

He puts them in his truck.

Cora is on a route.

She goes to
the same houses
each day.

Today she has
a package.

It is for Mr. Ross.

Bill sees a red flag.

There is mail to pick up!

He gets the mail.

Then he puts the flag down.

Deb works in a city.

She uses a cart.

She has a key to open mailboxes.

Art has a
mailbag.

mailbag ·········▶

18

He brings mail
to shops.

Mail carriers do good work!

At the Post Office

22

Picture Glossary

mailbag
A special bag where the mail carrier holds mail.

post office
A place where mail is sorted and people can send and pick up mail.

package
A box with something in it that someone mailed.

route
The places that a mail carrier brings mail to every day.

Index

To Learn More

Learning more is as easy as 1, 2, 3.

1) Go to www.factsurfer.com

2) Enter "mail carriers" into the search box.

3) Click the "Surf" button to see a list of websites.

With factsurfer.com, finding more information is just a click away.